Is He the One?

Is He the One?

101 Questions
That Will Lead You to the Truth,
Whatever That Is

Susan Swimmer

A Lark Production

**Andrews McMeel
Publishing**

Kansas City

Book design by Pete Lippincott

04 05 06 07 08 KP1 10 9 8 7 6 5 4 3 2 1

Library of Congress Cataloging-in-Publication Data

Swimmer, Susan.
   Is he the one? : 101 questions that will lead you to the truth, whatever that is / Susan Swimmer.
     p.cm.
  "A Lark Production"
  ISBN 0-7407-4194-2
   1. Mate selection. 2. Man-woman relationships. I. Title: 101 Questions that will lead you to the truth, whatever that is. II. Title.

HQ801.S95 2002
646.7'7—dc22

2003063858

ATTENTION: SCHOOLS AND BUSINESSES

For James,
the One

Introduction

FOR ANY WOMAN WHO'S LOOKING for The One, the journey to matrimony can be a tricky and treacherous course filled with hopes, expectations, and a few too many glasses of chardonnay. Finding the man you want to spend your life with begins and ends with a lot of little questions that add up to the big question: Is he the one?

Is He the One?: 101 Questions That Will Lead You to the Truth, Whatever That Is is the blueprint you need to figure out if you've found him. The questions? Crucial. The answers? Possibly life changing. Does he consider himself a lucky man? Are his criticisms of you constructive? Can he give up being right in a disagreement? Will he share his dessert in a restaurant?

This book is the ultimate heart-to-heart talk you need to have with yourself. Honest and enlightening, intimate and up-front, it's every girl's guide to finding long-lasting love. And best of all, when you get to the end of the book you'll actually be at the beginning, because whether it means you've decided to start anew or you are ready to say "I do," *Is He the One?* will lead you to the truth, whatever that is. 💌

Is He
the One?

When you give him a great smile, does he smile back?

AN EFFORTLESS, SINCERE SMILE is a little gift that you could be getting every single day. It tells you, in a nanosecond, that when you send him good vibes he's sending them right back at ya. Or not.

Is he proud of who he is?

WHETHER HE FEELS HE'S already the man he wants to be or he's still evolving into that person, he should be proud of the man he is today. Because really, if he's proud of *who* he is, then he knows *what* he is, and a healthy dose of self-realization is, well, healthy. Besides, even if he falls into the still-evolving category, odds are he'll get to where he wants to be eventually. And that's a ride you'll want to be along for.

*Can he tell the difference between a
serious problem and a minor irritation?*

THERE ARE SITUATIONS THAT ARE, in fact, challenging, and then there are problems that are actually just annoying little hassles. What you want is a man who can distinguish the two. A man who can tell the difference between the challenge-worthy issues and the stuff that's so small it's not worth much time and anxiety is someone who understands how to prioritize the obstacles that life has to offer. Getting laid off? A challenging problem. Out of milk and want a bowl of cereal? Annoying hassle. You get the picture.

*Do you know what he'd consider
his biggest fear?*

BEING ABLE TO REVEAL one's fear is scary in and of
itself. Having a *man* reveal fear is downright miraculous.
That said, if your man can do it, it shows that he feels
close enough *to* you and safe enough *with* you that he
can let himself look, act, and seem vulnerable. And that's
nothing to be afraid of.

Does he kiss you firmly?

A LISTLESS, UNCOMMITTED KISS is like a limp, clammy handshake (nice to meet you, *sort of*). Even the most gentle, tender kiss needs to feel like it knows where it's going.

Can he meet and hold your gaze?

IT WOULD BE GREAT to think that the glistening pools of your eyes are such an entrancing life force that they'd hold any man's gaze. Truth is, your gaze may not be all *that*, but it can be a pretty intense thing. Spend some face time with your man: While his averted gaze could indicate anything from a little insecurity to a lack of genuine interest, a gaze held is a promising sign of the trust, sincerity, and emotional connection you've been looking for.

Does he think he's a lucky guy?

YOU'D LIKE TO THINK that he is a man who understands that life is made up of part luck and part hard work, and that both elements will affect him at some point. A man who thinks himself lucky in any way is someone who radiates gratitude, which in turn creates an aura of joyousness. And that's all good. But what really matters is that, at the very least, he is a man who feels wildly fortunate to have *you* in his life, because a guy who feels that way will make sure you know you're adored. And how lucky is that?

Does he sigh a lot?

IF HE DOES, it's either a sign of a melancholy nature or a subtle form of nonverbal complaining. Either way it's something that could, in fact, become the negative background music to your entire relationship. Of course it could be a simple case of compensating for shallow breathing, which a little yoga could cure in a jiffy.

*Is he capable of not saying
anything at all while hugging?*

A MAN WHO CAN TOTALLY and completely lose himself
in a hug to the extent that it renders him speechless is a
good, soulful, loving man. And *that* is something you want.

Are his little faults things you can handle?

EVERYONE IS BUGGED by something. Does he drink directly from the carton? Hang sweaty clothes on the bathroom door? Stockpile old newspapers? Say no more. Ladies, there will *always* be habits that could drive you batty enough to head for the door, if you let them. But accepting someone, little faults and all, is part of love. You've got to think big picture here: Don't let his habit of rattling ice in a glass cloud your vision of a man who's caring, respectful, honest, and loving. And that's to say *nothing* of the fact that you crack your knuckles and leave half-empty coffee cups all over the house.

How quickly does he say "I'm sorry"?

SOMEWHERE BETWEEN IMMEDIATELY (ideal) and
twelve hours (plenty of time to think about it) is about
right. Being wrong is human, but apologizing for the
wrongdoing is the stuff men are made of. Real men.
Men who are mature and respectful and thoughtful and
caring. And that old adage about not going to bed angry
is true: If he waits more than twelve hours to say "I'm
sorry," then he's willing to let you lose sleep over it. And
that's just not nice.

Is he an original?

IF LIFE WITH HIM is a series of same old, same old, then it'll grow old, grow old. But if his idea of a great date is something other than dinner and a movie, if he sends you flowers and it's not a dozen red roses (and maybe he sends them and it's not even a real occasion), or if he writes his own message inside your birthday card, then this guy could very well be the real (original) deal.

Have you learned anything from him?

LIKE HOW TO GRILL SWORDFISH so it's crisp on the outside and juicy at the same time? Or get up on a sail-board without getting a swimsuit wedgie? Or play the harmonica so that your lips don't swell? If he's the one he'll want to teach you some of the things he loves, and you'll want to learn them, too.

*Does he know how to turn
a crying jag into a laughing fit?*

HE'D BETTER, because life is going to throw some doozies your way and if you don't have a man by your side who can make the best of it, even in the worst of it, then you run the risk of being overwhelmed by whatever "it" is. Getting through good times is easy; it's the hard times that require the help of a good mate.

15

*Can you name the parts of you
he finds most beautiful?*

IF YOU KNOW *right now,* without asking, that he loves
the small of your back, or the way your belly sort of bulges
when you lie on your side, or that your cheeks are the
softest part of your face, then he must have told you more
than once. And that's a beautiful thing.

When he has a piece of news,
does he call you first?

THE PECKING ORDER of news sharing is important, and don't let anyone tell you differently. When important stuff happens we all tend to think of our nearest and dearest first, right? So whether he got the promotion of a lifetime or his best friend ran off to Vegas to get married, it's nice to know that he wants to share it with you first.

Do you understand what it is about his best friend that he likes?

A PERSON'S BEST FRIEND says everything about the kind of person he's attracted to. Is he considerate? Generous? Kind? Loving? If you think his best friend is anything but a stand-up guy who brings out the best in your guy, then think again.

18

*Would he take the last sip of milk
for his morning coffee?*

EVEN IN A SLEEP-DEPRIVED, late for work, barely-able-to-
select-a-tie-stupor, the man who leaves *you* the last splash
of milk for your coffee is a man who understands consid-
eration. If he thinks to take your needs into account when
it comes to all of life's little "I'm thinking of you" gestures,
then he probably knows what they add up to.

Can he keep a secret?

NOT ALL SECRETS ARE THE SAME, and we all know that. Some are meant to be told and others are meant to be taken to the grave. That you got drunk one night might be a secret that gets told in the form of a funny story. That you have an STD might be one you'd like to take to the grave. What's most important is that the two of you categorize secrets, both large and small, in the same way.

*Does he act himself when
he's around your friends and family?*

IDEALLY, OF COURSE, you'd like him to rise to the occasion so much that he'd be the very best version of himself when he's with the people who matter to you the most. He'd be smart and warm and really clever *every single second*. But that's a lot of pressure for one guy. All you really need is a man who's strong enough to be himself, no matter whom he's with.

Does he anticipate your wishes?

ASIDE FROM THE FOLKS at Psychic Friends, no one can read minds. Still, some things are just obvious. Would he ward off a house full of poker-playing buddies on the night before your big presentation at work? Will he make you dinner the night you need it most? Let's hope so, because wanting a man who is thoughtful enough to anticipate your needs (especially when you need them the most) shouldn't be wishful thinking, it should be the way it is.

Is he generous with sweet talk?

COMPLIMENTS ARE LITTLE REMINDERS that he's thinking nice things about you, and handing them out happens easily when they come from the heart. As corny as it sounds, it's true. You can choose to hear nice things, you can choose to hear bad things, or you can choose to hear nothing at all. The choice is yours.

Will he share his dessert in a restaurant?

AS MUCH AS YOU WANT to understand a person who feels territorial about his dessert, any man who would deny you a couple of spoonfuls of something delicious would probably deny you all sorts of other things. And nobody should want to share in that.

10 Great Dates

DO YOU ACTUALLY WANT to have another evening of sitting and small talk? Didn't think so. Here are ten ideas that will tell you more than dinner and a movie.

1. *A museum.* He'd never think of it. See if he's willing to go for you. Besides, all those nudes have been exciting onlookers for ages.

2. *A picnic.* It's nice to know you can still have a great time even if you strip away all the comforts that a real restaurant can provide. He gets extra points if he brings along candles.

3. *A walk in the moonlight.* Or make it a run and benefit from all those endorphins.

4. *Partaking of some sport,* like racquetball or swimming. Now we're *really* talking endorphins.

5. *A phone date.* See if you still like talking to him once you take away the food, the entertainment, the ambience, and all the delicious physical contact.

6. *Volunteering.* Serve food at your local soup kitchen or help paint the gymnasium at the YMCA. If you want to see if a guy has heart, this is it.

7. *A road trip.* Go some place that's totally new and unfamiliar and discover something together.

8. *Baby-sitting.* Nothing like a needy, sometimes irritable child to test his humor *and* his humility.

9. *Cooking a meal together.* Whether it's something that a master chef would create or spaghetti and meatballs, cooking a meal takes time, good communication, and the use of really sharp knives. See if you can create something yummy together and not want to stab each other by the end of it.

10. *Skinny-dipping.* Nothing says "totally comfortable" like being soaking wet and completely naked.

Do you know how much money he has?

NOT TO THE PENNY, but a ballpark figure. And here's the catch: You should know because the two of you have discussed it openly and honestly, not because you surreptitiously accessed his computer files while he was grilling out back.

*Does he share the love of your
four-legged friends?*

THE FACT THAT HE DOESN'T actually want Fluffy in bed with the two of you all the time should not worry you. Men never understand that a warm, furry, four-legged friend could be more appealing than, say, a man, and they never will. But at the very least he should adhere to the if-you-love-it-then-I-love-it philosophy, and he should also offer to clean up the occasional accident.

Do you accept and accommodate his pastimes?

KEEP IN MIND THAT A MAN without a pastime is a man
who spends too much time in the house. That said, you
should *each* accommodate the other's pastimes, without
harsh judgment or a mental stopwatch (how long does it
take to play eighteen holes of golf?). Time apart is normal,
time apart is healthy, and time apart lets you spend an
entire Saturday afternoon shopping for shoes and talking
about George Clooney's *very* cute ass. And that, my friend,
is time well spent.

*Does he love his work or have some
other passion to which he is dedicated?*

DOING SOMETHING that you feel passionate about
reminds you of your reason for being. For some it's a job
they love, but for others it's a hobby or a charity or a place
or a person. It's something that inspires excitement and
commitment, and you want a man who not only understands this but who also feels it firsthand. Indifference and
apathy? Bad. Enthusiasm and dedication? Good.

Can he give up being right in a disagreement?

COUPLES WHO NEVER FIGHT are imaginary. Every couple disagrees from time to time, from the age-old cap off the toothpaste to where to buy a house. Knowing how to fight is important, but knowing how to stop fighting is more important. A good man knows how to give up being right, and a great man will do it periodically even when he *is* right.

Do you know about every important relationship he's had?

HIS PAST RELATIONSHIPS are the path that he took to get to you. They reflected his interests, shaped his expectations, and, for better or for worse, met his needs. And that means something. Skip the gory details (you don't really need to know where they had sex for the first time, do you?) and find out what those experiences meant to him. Whether it's his high school sweetheart or the spring fling he had in '93, the women who left an imprint, emotionally, spiritually, psychologically, or otherwise, are important women to get to know.

*Do you appreciate what he saw
in his ex-girlfriends?*

NO ONE'S SUGGESTING that you should like this cast of characters so much that you'd invite them all over for a hot meal and a round of charades. But realize this: The relationships he's had are living examples of what he looks for in a mate. If you can't respect him for the really important choices he's made in the past, then how can you trust the choice he's making in you?

Does he work on who he is as a person?

NO MATTER HOW OLD YOU ARE or where you are in your life, rethinking your own evolution is downright healthy. If you've got a man who's willing (not to mention able) to stand back and reassess, then by all means cherish him. Now if he hires a spiritual adviser and can't tear himself away from his gratitude journal, then perhaps he needs a *little* less Oprah.

32

*Is he at ease with you,
whether you're alone or with friends?*

THE COMFORT LEVEL he has with you should be constant in your relationship. Whether you're alone, with a couple of friends, or in a mosh pit, you should feel comfortable with each other.

Are his criticisms of you constructive?

YOU CAN CHOOSE TO LIVE in a partnership with a man who helps and supports you and, yes, offers helpful criticism when you need it most, or you can live with someone who cuts you down to keep you in your place because he needs to overcompensate for what *has* to be a *tiny* penis. You decide.

34

*Can he happily spend an evening
alone with you without having sex?*

AN EVENING WITHOUT SEX is like an evening . . . without sex. For the young or newly in love this may seem crazy, but believe this: What with kids, careers, and a myriad of commitments, a night or two without sex is going to sound pretty good. You want to be with a man who has the legs (and the libido) to stand up to a night that's fornication-free.

*Do you know how he handles
the money he makes?*

FIGHTING OVER MONEY is practically an American
pastime. That said, figuring out how your man makes it,
spends it, and saves it is important. It doesn't matter if he's
a gazillionaire or a minimum wager, what makes all the
difference is how he handles what he has. You want a guy
who works honestly, saves responsibly, and spends sensibly.
He should be a stranger to neither generosity nor frugality,
but rather a man who understands that life will provide
times for both.

10 Things That Tell You Nothing About a Man

IF YOU WANT TO GET TO THE BOTTOM of his character, to who he is as a man, then you're going to have to dig a little deeper than this.

1. *You have a great time partying.* Well, let's hope so! Jack the Ripper and Pol Pot would have a good time partying, but you wouldn't have wanted to be married to either one.

2. *You have mind-blowing sex. Every* couple is two margaritas short of mind-blowing sex. Do you still love him when the sex is just so-so?

3. *He has a great job.* If anything comes and goes these days, it's a good job. Can he be kind and loving without the corner office?

4. *He has a lot of money.* No matter what anybody tells you, at the end of the day you can't curl up with a wad of cash and feel loved.

5. *He's never been in therapy.* Lots of people haven't been in therapy, but that doesn't mean they haven't needed it.

6. *You've known each other for a really long time.* It's not *that* you know him, it's *what* you know of him.

7. *Your grandmother thinks he's perfect.* That he can impress your grandmother is a measure of manners, not a man.

8. *He's great looking.* That he's won the handsome-gene lottery makes him a lucky guy. What else can you tell your friends about him?

9. *He's got an amazing wardrobe.* The only thing this tells you is that he (or his last girlfriend) knows how to shop. Interesting, but not terribly important.

10. *He pays for everything.* This is also known as a business relationship—possibly the oldest business in the world.

36

Has he seen you when you're at your worst?

WORSE THAN NO MAKEUP. Beyond bad hair. We're talking about the really evil side of you that's a brutal cocktail of bitter depression, stunning irritability, and Olympic-level bitchiness. It's the you that *nobody* should be subjected to. You know the you we're talking about here. Yes, *that one*. If he's seen *that* you and he can handle it without calling 911, then he may be a keeper.

Have you ever suspected him of lying?

FIRST OF ALL, take out of this equation all the little "white lies" that he may tell. ("Of course you don't look fat in that." "Your mother isn't at all intrusive.") What's at issue here are the big, ugly, hurtful lies that matter, and it's really quite simple. If you suspect he's lied, then the relationship is already in trouble because suspicion is the first step in eroding trust. No trust? No chance.

Can you explain what he does for a living?

YOU SHOULD BE ABLE TO EXPLAIN his work because it should matter to you. Not in excruciating detail, not with manual-worthy accuracy, but with enough familiarity that it's clear that you get it. And if you can't explain it, then you're probably not listening or not interested (or both), and that won't really work for anyone.

*Do you know what he'd consider
the best experience of his life?*

SO HE HASN'T CLIMBED MT. EVEREST, sung at the
Grammys, or slept at the White House. Regardless, he
should, at the very least, be able to describe a couple of
really great experiences that have had a huge effect on his
life. A long-lasting effect. Maybe even lifelong lasting.
Because really, the best experiences in his life have shaped
him, and don't you want to know what shape that is?

10 Test Scenarios

THESE ARE A FEW REAL-DEAL EXPERIENCES that a healthy, strong relationship can endure.

1. *The Family Dinner.* If breaking bread makes you think of breaking up, then perhaps you've got too much on your plate.

2. *The Weeklong Trip.* You won't find this in the vacation brochure, but taking a trip together isn't just fun in the sun—it often requires patience, compromise, and lots of communication.

3. *The "Let's Try Something New."* If you find yourself thinking "If the parasail doesn't kill him, I will," then perhaps this man's not for you.

4. *The Big Purchase.* Averting a blow-up when you're about to break the bank will prepare you for things like home ownership, your kid's college tuition, and the occasional spa vacation.

5. *The Handling of a Crisis.* You have to know you can keep it together when it feels like the world is falling apart.

6. *The Death in the Family.* Sad times call for strong bonds, and it's as simple as that.

7. *The Big Life Change.* Whether it's a new job, a new home, or a whole new outlook, weathering change is a challenge he needs to meet.

8. *The Best Friend's Wedding.* It could be an evening filled with insecurity, jealousy, and unrealistic expectations, or it could just be a rocking good time. It's up to you.

9. *The Office Party.* Crackers with coworkers is harder than it sounds. Make sure you've got a man who can stand by your side without making a scene.

10. *The Relocation.* Whether you're moving to a new zip code or a new time zone, you should still be able to meet in the middle.

Does he know your hairdresser's name?

BARRING SOME UNBELIEVABLE COINCIDENCE (like that they actually have the same name), it's a rare man who knows this sort of information. It would be wonderful to think that you're with a guy who so eagerly hangs on every word you say that he picks up on minutia such as this, but a deal breaker it's not. What matters is that he's willing to learn whatever it is that's truly important to you. Besides, he should be saving room for more pertinent information, like the name of your jeweler.

Does he see the humor in life?

BEING ABLE TO STAND BACK and simply laugh at a situation that truly warrants it is a gift, because life really is funny sometimes. Any marriage will see its fair share of trouble and aggravation, and having a partner who can ease the angst with a little bit of humor will go a long way.

*Is his relationship with his family
something you can live with?*

THESE DAYS ESPECIALLY, families are *complicated*. It is a
rare brood of parents and siblings and step-everythings that
live in harmony. The amount of time and energy people
devote to their families varies, from all the time to no time
at all. Those twice-weekly dinners at his mother's house
may seem fun at first, but after six months you might find
yourself wishing he were an orphan. Figure out how
much togetherness is the right amount for you, and then
make a plan you can both live with. If you can't agree or
negotiate the difference, then maybe he's not the one
for you.

Is he comfortable caring for a baby?

IF HE IS, GREAT, if he's not, don't sweat it. Historically, serious baby caring has always fallen into the domain of women's work. Many, many great men have been chased away from cribs and changing tables the world over. What matters most is that he's willing to try and eager to learn.

*Do you often feel the need
to make excuses for him?*

IF YOU FIND YOURSELF STUCK for an explanation as
to why he's rude to your family, antisocial toward your
friends, or obnoxious to you, then maybe you've got a
guy who's rude, antisocial, and obnoxious. You may need
a lot of things in your life, but a man you need to make
excuses for is not one of them.

Do you know what he values most?

A MAN WHO HAS FIGURED OUT what he truly values in his life understands the difference between the stuff that really matters and the stuff that's just nice to have. A new car with leather interior? Nice to have. A woman like you? An irreplaceable value. Find a man who knows the difference and it'll make a *big* difference to you.

46

Does he surprise you?

WITH A PRESENT when it's not an occasion, or with a letter that he wrote and sent in the mail, or by telling you you're beautiful when you think you look your worst? Surprises are the spice of life, and unless you're looking for a relationship with no taste, you want a man who knows how to add a little flavor now and then.

*Does he give of himself, either
in time or money?*

A GIVING MAN IS A GOOD MAN, and it's as simple as that.

48

Does he know the things he's good at?

THERE ARE CERTAIN REALIZATIONS that come with maturity, and knowing what you're good at is one of them. A man who recognizes his assets while accepting his limitations is someone who simply "gets it." What's more, if his expectations of himself are realistic, then his expectations of you are likely to be that way, too.

If he could live anyplace,
do you know where that would be?

WHETHER IT'S AROUND THE CORNER or around the globe, what matters is that he's factoring you, your needs, your lifestyle, and all of your stuff into the floor plan in his mind.

*Does he introduce you to all the
important people in his life?*

NICE, LOVING, HONEST PEOPLE surround themselves
with people of the same nature, and mean, thoughtless,
arrogant people do the same. A man's inner circle speaks
volumes about who he is as a person. Your man should
want to share with you the people in his life who make
a difference to him because they are a part of who he is,
and he should also want to share you with them for the
same reason.

If he found a dishwasher filled with clean dishes, would he empty it?

OR WIPE SPILLED COFFEE off the counter? Or replace an empty roll of toilet paper? Your man may not embrace housework with as much time or gusto as you do, but a man who won't even clean up what he spills may have failed (your) home economics for the last time.

*How does he treat people who
wait on him in restaurants?*

HOPEFULLY IT IS WITH THE UTMOST RESPECT, because
anything but that is unacceptable. And a generous tipper
never hurts.

*Do you know the one thing
he'd change about himself if he could?*

YES, CHANGE IS GOOD. A first-rate man is someone who doesn't stand still in *any* phase in his life but rather continues to evolve. Would you have fallen in love with his twelve-year-old self? Not likely, unless you were contemplating a union with a guy who worshiped Ring Dings and collected comic books. And he should *still* be evolving, even now. A man who isn't afraid to take a look at who he is and see that he's due for a change is a man who's not afraid of change.

Does he tell you he loves you
on a regular basis?

NOT BECAUSE YOU ASK HIM, or beg him, or only after sex. He should tell you often because he knows how good it feels to hear those words and because it feels good to say them.

*When you have an argument,
do you feel you are heard?*

WHAT'S THE ESSENCE of every successful relationship?
Communication. The road to a happy relationship is one
paved with respect and understanding, even in times of
disagreement. What makes arguments so constructive is
that they enable you to get the bad feelings out in order to
move on to a better place. If you don't feel like you're
heard, you'll feel like you're being steamrolled.

10 Relationship Myths

1. *The sex is never as good as it is in the beginning.* You may not be doing it five times a day, but if you put your mind (and body) to it, you can *always* have great sex.

2. *The sex only gets better.* In movies, sure, but in real life, where there are jobs and kids and all sorts of sleep-depriving responsibilities, hot sex often (but not always—see #1) has to compete for equal time.

3. *He'll change.* Hair color changes, traffic lights change, but men, they can't be counted on to change. That's not true. They change the channel all the time.

4. *He'll never change.* Never say never: Given the right set of circumstances (an ultimatum and possibly a miracle) anyone can change. Yes, *even men.*

5. *When you marry the man you marry the family.*
   Actually, you marry the *relationship* he has with his family. If your man only sees his family once in a blue barbecue, then perhaps their effect on you will be negligible. But if his mother is still cutting up his nightly meat, good luck prying the knife out of her hand.

6. *The key to a good relationship is never to go to bed angry.*
   It's a lovely sentiment, but things like trust, communication, compatibility, and, um, *love* are probably more the keys to a long-lasting union.

7. *The way he treats his mother is the way he'll treat you.*
   The way he treats his mother *is the way he treats his mother*. Spend your time thinking about the way he treats *you*.

8. *You've got to date a lot of men to find the one.* Finding the right one only requires that you are able to recognize him when you meet him, whether he's the first or the four hundredth.

9. *There's only one true love for every person.* There are 6.4 billion people in the world and you think there's only one for you? Odds are good that you didn't score so well on your probability and statistics test in high school.

10. *All men have a fear of commitment.* There's nothing that *all* men think or feel. When he says he has a fear of commitment, what he's really saying is that he has a fear of commitment to *you.* Harsh but true.

Does he often keep you waiting?

HIS KEEPING YOU STANDING on a street corner or sitting quietly alone at a table for two should be such an infrequent occurrence that he shouldn't have a usual way of explaining it. It shows a complete disregard for you and your time. It's selfish, and it's just plain bad manners. Look, traffic happens, but at the very least he should apologize profusely, shower you with kindness, and have a better excuse than "the dog ate my wristwatch."

Does he admit the things he's bad at?

LIKE THAT HE CAN'T FIX THINGS around the house, or buy appropriate gifts for people, or navigate directions when he's driving? It's called humility, and having it makes a good man grateful for what he *can* do.

*Do you know whom he trusts
most in his life?*

THESE ARE THE PEOPLE he goes to for help, advice,
inspiration, and a little cash when times get tough.
They're the ones with the opinions that matter most to
him. You want to know who these people are, and you
want to know that you're one of them.

*If he had to give up his career,
do you know what else he'd want to do?*

THE THING TO REMEMBER about true love for another
person is that it is just that: You love the person, not his
bank account, his job, or any of his circumstances. Because
as we all know, circumstances change. Try out a few what-
if scenarios and see how it feels. What if he ran for public
office? Or joined the Peace Corps? Or moved to Montana
to try his hand at ranching? If you can't accept the what-if
scenarios, then you can't happily live in the here-and-now
realities.

Is he liked by the people who work for him?

MEN WHO ARE UNIVERSALLY LOATHED by the people who work for them are rarely simply misunderstood. Being deeply disliked is earned by being truly awful. When you're the boss, it's sometimes tricky. When your man is in charge, if he's able to strike a balance between being a disciplined taskmaster and a respected human being then it's something that must matter to him. And *that* is a good thing.

*If he were to run from a burning building,
do you know what he'd take?*

HE'S GOING TO GRAB the things that matter to him
most. You should know him well enough to know what
he'd grab, and when you consider his choices you should
love him even more. There are men who'd rescue a cat,
or a collection of family photographs, or the book a great-
grandfather has left behind . . . and then there are the
guys who'd save their stereos.

*Do you find him attractive
even at those times when he's not?*

IF YOU THINK HE LOOKS A LITTLE RAGGED after a
fishing trip with the guys (to say nothing of the way he
smells), then listen up: It's the really tough times that test
a man's place on the attract-o-meter. He'll always be
attractive after a shower and a shave, but if you're still
digging him when he's hurt, angry, sick, unemployed,
desperate, and helpless, then perhaps it's love.

Will he try something new, like a food or a sport, without putting up a fight?

HERE'S WHAT REALLY separates man from dog: You *can* teach a man, young or old, new tricks. Any man who's unwilling or unable to try something new every now and again should be put in the pound.

When you go to a party,
is he the one you want to go home with?

THERE'S NOTHING WRONG with looking, ogling, even fantasizing every now and then about other men. But at the end of the night the man you choose should always be the man you'd choose. After all, if you can't enjoy your party of two, then maybe you've got the wrong guest list.

*Does he give you time to pursue
the things that interest you?*

HE DOESN'T HAVE TO passionately embrace your love
of Impressionist art, he doesn't even necessarily have to
look at a single picture of a sunset over Provence, but he
needs to respect that it's of interest to you. So maybe he
doesn't want to spend an entire day museum hopping, or
wandering around a flea market, or planting gladiolas.
What's important is that he gives you the time and the
space, without the grief or the guilt, to do it yourself.

Are you comfortable with
the way he observes his religion?

THE SUBJECT OF RELIGION has busted many a strong bond. Hell, entire civilizations have gone down because of it. Whether he's estranged from all things organized or has decided to become the grand pooh-bah in the Church of Chocolate, his religious affiliation is something you need to respect, not rebuff, if you want the civilization of the two of you to survive.

*Are you on the same page
when it comes to having children?*

MANY A COUPLE have walked down the aisle, seemingly
safe in the knowledge that they know they want a family.
But unless you've talked specifics, that's like saying you'll
never have to worry about cooking because you both like
to eat. Who's going to make the meal? What's it going to
be? When will it be served? Who will take care of that
meal when both of you want to continue climbing the
corporate ladder but neither of you likes the idea of paid
food care?

*Do you ever feel he pushes you to do
something that makes you feel uncomfortable?*

RELATIONSHIPS ARE MADE UP of lots of compromises.
Sometimes you give a little, sometimes he gives a little.
It's the law of the relationship jungle. What a healthy
relationship shouldn't require is the abandonment of
your inner compass, that tiny device inside your brain
that tells you what feels right to you. If you can't be true
to yourself and be true to him at the same time, then
maybe it's not true love.

Do you know where he sees himself in fifteen years?

IN SUCH AND SUCH A JOB, living in such and such a place, in such and such a kind of house. Blah, blah, blah. If his designs on his future go too far without mentioning you and the life you want to live, then in fifteen years' time he may be living solo.

Can he nurse himself back from a cold?

KITTENS ARE CUTE when they're helpless; men are not. A guy who can't get himself over the common cold (we're talking about a little extra sleep, a couple of aspirin, and lots of liquids) will be unable to handle all sorts of tiny setbacks. And that's to say nothing of something big like, say, surgery. Don't let his sickness ruin your health.

Does he wear a seatbelt?

WEARING A SEATBELT is a tiny gesture that says he cares about himself and his well-being. Like eating vegetables. Or wearing sunscreen. Takes a minute, lasts a lifetime.

72

*Is it easy or hard to rent a movie
that you'd both want to watch?*

IF YOU HAVE TO GO FOUR ROUNDS before you angrily
rent two movies (one for you, one for him), then you are
absolutely expending too much energy on the small stuff.
A marriage is like a decision-making marathon: You need
to conserve your time and enthusiasm for when you really
need it, or you'll never finish the race.

*Do you like the person he is
when he's "with the guys"?*

THE MAN HE IS when he's with "the guys," the cigar-smoking, poker-playing, bad-joke-telling guy who only seems to come out when tipped off by other testosterone, is in fact one piece of his personality puzzle. You may not *love* that side of him, but it shouldn't be so awful that it offends you or scares you or makes you want to leave with no forwarding address.

Does he control his temper?

CONTROLLING ONE'S TEMPER doesn't mean not getting angry. Everyone gets angry. You actually want a man who gets his undies in a bunch every now and then, because it tells you he's got feelings, even bad ones, that are passionate enough to get the old blood boiling. But make sure he's the sort of guy who can get his point across without blowing his lid.

10 Reasons to Walk

WHY BAD RELATIONSHIPS HAPPEN to good women is a question for the ages. Here are ten telltale signs that say *stop*.

1. He's abusive.
2. He's controlled by his addictions.
3. He wants you to change your appearance.
4. He lies.
5. He doesn't respect your family.
6. He doesn't like any of your friends.
7. He criticizes you more than he praises you.
8. He doesn't respect what you do for a living.
9. He's a control freak.
10. He's married.

Do the people you trust the most think he's a good guy?

YOUR FRIENDS, your family, and the people closest to you are your very own truth testers: They look out for your interests and steer you right when you veer off course. If those important people in your life can't understand what you see in him, then maybe you need to take a second look.

Does he take responsibility for his actions?

THERE ARE THE BIG ACTIONS he takes, like deciding to leave his job, and then there are the not-so-big ones, like deciding to eat dessert before dinner. A good, strong man knows that taking responsibility for one's actions is the hallmark of maturity. If he can do that then he can have his dessert and eat it, too.

*You go on vacation together and
hit seven days of rain. Can he deal?*

THERE ARE THINGS IN LIFE that you just can't plan.
Disappointments are unavoidable, accidents happen, and
weather is unpredictable. Life is loopy that way. You can
choose to be with a guy who caves in the face of misfor-
tune, or you can choose to be with a man who makes
the best of it. Choose wisely.

78

*Can you disagree with each other
and not have a big fight?*

THERE ARE CERTAINLY ISSUES that will be worth a
knockdown, drag-out fight (like that you've spent the rent
money on two pairs of Manolos), and then there are the
trillion little negotiations that have to happen on a weekly
basis in order to keep the relationship running, like where
to hang a picture or who should fold the laundry. Not
only do you want a guy who can fight nice, but you also
want someone who can differentiate the basics from the
big deal.

*Are you able to tell each other
what you want in bed?*

MIND READING IN THE BEDROOM is a fantasy; your sex
life should be a reality. It doesn't matter if you like hanging from the ceiling or doing the missionary mambo night
after night. What's important is that you and your man are
able to talk openly so that you may get, give, and groove
on what each other wants, needs, and craves.

Does he know how to make a child laugh?

SHORT OF A MEMORY BANK full of knock-knock jokes, knowing how to make a child laugh can be a mysterious thing. For the childless, it takes time, patience, and a supreme lack of self-consciousness. Any man who's actually willing to make fish faces, stand on his head, and belch the alphabet is a man who's in touch with his inner child. And who wouldn't want to play with that?

Would he help a stranger in need?

THERE IS SOMETHING almost old-fashioned about the sort of man who helps a complete stranger carry a heavy load, make change for the bus, or find his way when lost. Sad, no? Common decency shouldn't go the way of the old and outdated. A man who's willing to do the little things it takes to make life for others a tiny bit better is a kind and thoughtful guy. And that never goes out of style.

*Does he respect the time
you want to spend with your family?*

THERE'S A RHYTHM to the way you interact with your parents and siblings. It's . . . familiar. While it's certainly normal to make *some* changes when you add a mate, the addition shouldn't change *everything*. If you're forced to choose between him and them, you'll probably lose both.

*Do you accept the amount of time
he spends apart from you?*

SOME COUPLES live in harmony bicoastally, and some like to be joined at the hip. Whether he spends long hours at work, on the golf course, or carousing with his buddies when you're apart is not the point. If you feel he's taking time *away* from you, then he may not be the man *for* you.

*Do you feel he loves you
even when you've screwed something up?*

IT'S EASY FOR A MAN to love and adore you when
you're providing him with sparkling conversation while
cooking his favorite dinner . . . in the nude. It takes a
great man to feel the love even after you've inadvertently
insulted his boss or accidentally scratched his new car.

*If he won a hundred thousand dollars,
do you know how he'd spend it?*

IT DOESN'T MATTER if he'd invest it all in treasury
bonds or blow the entire wad on black 27. What matters
most is that you're able to love and support the man who
makes the choice, whatever it is.

Do the two of you have a world together that's yours and nobody else's?

YOU'D LIKE TO THINK that the two of you are building a little world together, a world that's separate from the big world around you. And inside that little world he feels safe enough to share his innermost thoughts. Like his ultimate truths, dreamy expectations, unexplained questions, and maybe even a fantasy or two. If he isn't interested in the world of the two of you, then maybe you're better off in your world of one.

*Would he go to couple's therapy
if you wanted him to?*

THERE ARE MANY EXCUSES he can use to avoid counseling: He's not comfortable talking to a stranger, he doesn't have the time, it's not his style, it's a waste of money, and on and on. But a little therapy is a great tool to have in your relationship toolbox if need be. If he's really in love with you then a little counseling now and then shouldn't spook him. A good man knows that anything is worth a try when it comes to helping, even saving, your relationship.

Can he laugh at himself?

HUMOR CAN GET YOU THROUGH a lot of tough times. There are those who don't laugh at all, those who laugh easily at others, and then those who have the strong sense of self, not to mention the maturity, to laugh at themselves.

*Do you feel he makes time for you
when you need it?*

IT DOESN'T MATTER what kind of deadline he has at work, which play-off game the tickets are for, or who just happens to be in town for one night. There are a million things he *could* be doing, *should* be doing, or would *like* to be doing, but if he's not there for you when you need him, then who needs him?

Is he good in a crisis?

YOU AND HE MAY NEVER face a single crisis. That would make you very fortunate and possibly from another planet. Life happens, and some of it is bad and sudden and tests your ability to handle what comes your way. Being able to rise to the occasion, good, bad, or otherwise, without freaking out or running for the door (or both), is what men are made of. And that includes killing the big ugly bugs in the bathtub.

*Do you ever have trouble
explaining his behavior?*

IT DOESN'T MATTER if he likes to bark at the moon,
skip to work, or wear plaid briefs, as long as his behavior
makes sense to you.

Can he go along to get along?

LIKE TO THAT electricity-free macrobiotic restaurant you've been curious about, or the French film festival, or to a friend's wedding on, say, the night of the Super Bowl? The point is that a good man is able to put aside his own meat-eating, subtitle-hating, football-obsessed needs when it *really* matters to you, without a bribe or a big fight. And he should do it before he's legally bound.

93

Will he hold his ground when he's committed to something?

A MAN WHO *always* holds his own interests at heart is selfish, and a man who *always* puts aside his own agenda for others has lost his sense of self. He should be able to give up his ground some of the time, and he should be able to hold his ground some of the time, and he should be able to let you do the same.

*Are his housekeeping habits
something you can live with?*

A MAN WHO HAS SPENT his entire life living with wet towels balled up on the floor will not, upon uttering the words "I do," start folding them in thirds and hanging them to dry. And for the record, you're not going to change your ways, either. Split up the household chores so each of you is responsible for what matters to you the most (whoever thinks an unmade bed is unimaginable is the one who should make it), and split the difference with as much hired help as you can afford.

10 Statistics to Commit to Memory

IT SEEMS THAT LOVE IS IN THE AIR *and* in the numbers. Here are a few sobering statistics to commit to your pre-marital memory.

1. Think you'll never find him? Guess again: Singles constitute more than 40 percent of the adult population.

2. For those who did take a trip down the aisle, only 15 percent surveyed said they knew they were in love with their spouse when they first met him or her.

3. But maybe wisdom comes with age: The average age of the first marriage is twenty-five for women and almost twenty-seven for men.

4. Today in the United States, one in three single women chooses to live with her partner before marriage, and, *ahem*, attention women who wait: The majority of cohabiters either move out or marry within two years.

5. What does it take to make it last? Magic, schmagic: 86 percent of married couples believe that compromise and negotiation play a bigger role in keeping their partnership alive than chemistry and magic.

6. There's sex, too. The U.S. average for the frequency of sex is 124 days per year. Couples who are living together but not married are the most sexually active—they make love 145 times a year, as compared to singles who are not in a steady relationship, who have sex 86 times a year.

7. And, paging all cheating hearts: 75 percent of married men and 85 percent of married women surveyed say they *have* been faithful.

8. But, alas, divorce happens. In fact, 49 percent of couples who've been recently married reported that they're already having serious marital problems. What's more, five out of ten first marriages may eventually end in divorce, and of first marriages that do end in divorce, many end in the first three to five years.

9. And if you think shacking up is a great test run, you're wrong. Those who live together before marriage are almost twice as likely to divorce as those who do not live together.

10. One last thought before you call the caterer: The average two-hundred-guest wedding costs between fifteen thousand and thirty thousand dollars.

Sources: U.S. Bureau of the Census, 1992, 2000; Larry L. Bumpass & James A. Sweet, "National Estimates of Cohabitation," 1989; Michael, Gagnon, Laumann, and Kolata, *Sex in America: A Definitive Study* (Little, Brown, and Company); The Alan Guttmacher Institute, "In Their Own Right: Addressing the Sexual and Reproductive Health Needs of American Men," 2002; David Whitman, "Was It Good for Us?," *U.S. News and World Report,* May 19, 1997; Drs. Les and Leslie Parrott, *Saving Your Marriage Before It Starts* (Zondervan/Harpercollins); Match.com, Survey of Married Couples, 2003; The Durex Global Sex Survey, 2001.

95

*Are you happy with
the way you make decisions together?*

BEING ONE HALF of a couple is all about teamwork, most
especially when it comes to making decisions. Whether
it's where to live, who gets to go to graduate school, or
whether you're joining a church or a synagogue, if you've
ever felt subjugated, ignored, coerced, or browbeaten by
the man who claims he's your partner, then perhaps
there's one more decision you need to make.

Do you feel you can tell him anything?

YOU SHOULD FEEL so completely comfortable and at ease with him that you could tell him *anything*, but that doesn't mean you have to tell him *everything*.

*Is he helpful and sympathetic
when you're in pain?*

THE BEST (and possibly only) way to test out whether he'll be able to handle real pain—whether the physical pain testers like childbirth or the emotional doozies like the loss of a loved one—is to feel sure that he can handle the small stuff. A man who runs for the door at the mere mention of depression, who balks at a Band-Aid, or thinks period cramps are an urban myth will never be there for you when you need him most.

Is he fun?

A FUN MAN is someone who enjoys life. He laughs at
jokes, enjoys a good meal, finds entertainment, and dances
when the mood strikes. There's a certain youthful lightness
to a man who's fun, because he knows how to live in the
moment—he takes a good look at his surroundings, sees
the potential, and partakes of the possibilities. Now *that*
sounds like fun.

Is he affectionate?

A TENDER TOUCH, a warm kiss, a gentle rub. These are things you should receive every single day. And you shouldn't have to ask.

*Do you feel like he always
puts you in the best light?*

A GOOD, THOUGHTFUL, gracious man will always put
you in the best light, not because you don't have flaws,
because the truth is you do, but because he *chooses* to see
the good. Whether you've put on a few pounds, forgotten
a friend's birthday, or missed an opportunity to shine at
work, you want to be with a man who sees it, accepts it,
and moves beyond it. Because after all, making sure you
feel good about yourself shouldn't be a problem for him, it
should be a pleasure.

*Would you marry him
even if there were no reception,
no party, no nothing?*

IF YOU DESIGNED your wedding dress in grade school,
own a collection of bridal magazines, and worship at the
altar of WeddingChannel.com, then get a grip. A wedding
party lasts *one* day, but a marriage should be forever. If the
fantasy is ruined once the party is pooped, then maybe
you're dreaming of the wrong event.